WEIRDO 4

SUPER WEIRD!

ISBN 978-93-5471-089-6
First U.S. printing 2019
This edition : May 2022

Typeset in Chaloops Senior, Push Ups, and Lunch Box

Printed at Sterling Graphics Pvt. Ltd., Manesar

ANH DO

Illustrated by JULES FABER

WEiRDO 4

SUPER WEIRD!

SCHOLASTIC INC.

SUPER SAUSAGE

CHAPTER 1

You already know that me and my family are a **bit** weird!

But guess what? Our new puppy, FiDo, is **WEIRD**, too!

FiDo's a sausage dog. He has **super-short legs** and a **super-looooooooong** body.

He can't jump very high, but he can **wriggle-under** almost anything!

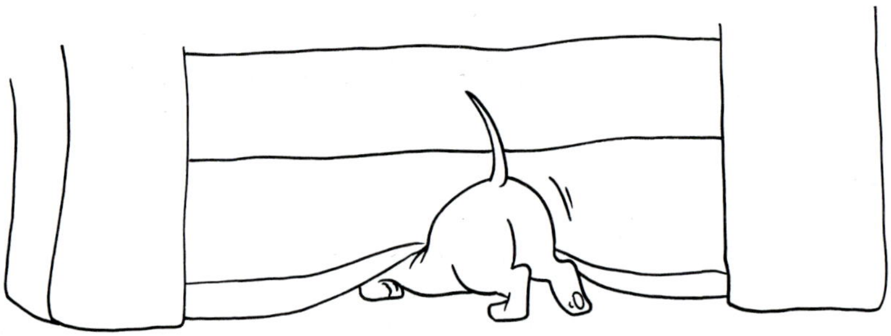

He keeps wriggling into **weird** places and finding things we haven't seen in **aaaaaaaaaaaages!**

Like Sally's **socks** . . .

And Dad's **gadgets** . . .

Roger's **pacifier** . . .

And Granddad's **teeth!**

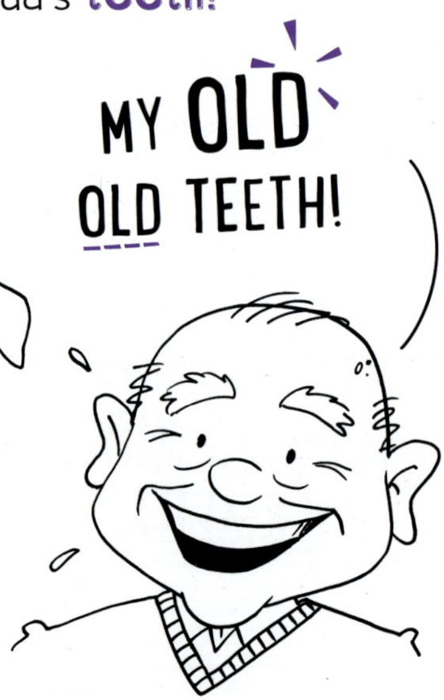

FiDo's **really** brave. He's not scared of anything.

He's like a **SUPER** sausage dog.

IS IT A DOG? IS IT A SAUSAGE?
NO, IT'S **SUPER** SAUSAGE DOG!

Faster than a **speeding bullfrog!**

More **powerful** than a **crazy chicken!**

Able to get under **anything** in a single crawl!

In fact, both of our pets are **really brave**. Blockhead isn't scared of anything, either. He's like the **bravest parrot** in town!

He's so brave, they should name a **bravery award** after him.

Oh, I forgot . . .

Blockhead **IS** scared of one thing.

Just one thing.

Flashing lights!

But that's nothing, really.

Blockhead and FiDo have become **best friends**.

They **sing** together.

They **sleep** together.

They practice **barking** together.

They even watch funny TV shows together.

Their favorite TV show is called *Funniest Pets*. People send in videos of their pets doing funny things!

Blockhead and **FiDo** do **tons** of funny things, too. They like to run around together like this

It's **SO funny** watching them **ride around** like that!

FiDo's not very fast, 'cause of his **little legs**. But that's kind of why I like him **even more!**

I'm **short** and **can't run very fast**, either!

Perfect!

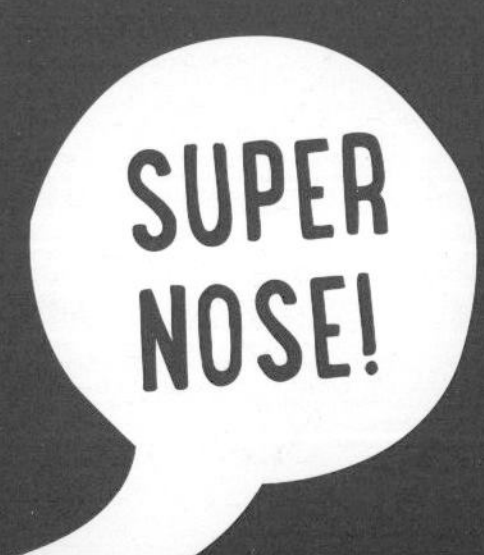
SUPER
NOSE!

CHAPTER 2

I guess everyone has something they are good at (even me!). And my dad is **reeeeeeally good** at **SMELLING things**.

It's like he's a **superhero**,

and **smelling things** is his **superpower!**

It would be **great** if he could
use his power to fight crime!

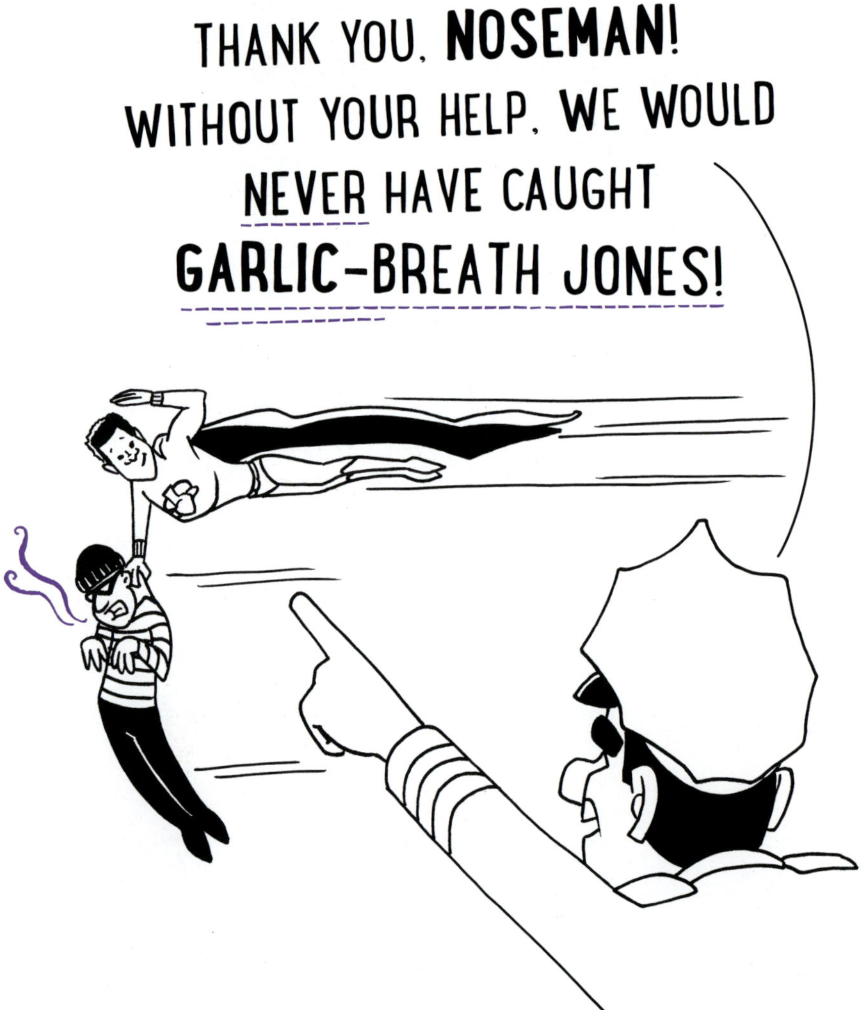

If you talk to Dad for a bit, **he can tell what you ate** for breakfast!

ME?
GREEN APPLE,
A TUB OF YOGURT . . .
AND A HANDFUL
OF DIRT!
WOW!

MEOW, MEOW,
MOO?
BIRDSEED!
WOOF!
(I told you Blockhead
was weird!)

He can even tell what **FiDo's** eaten!

Dad says it's because he has

a GREAT nose.

He's **SO good** at smelling things that he can **smell smoke** from a **loooooooong way away.**

He's always ready to **leap** into action as soon as he smells smoke in the air. He's had a few **false alarms**, but he always says it's

better to be

safe than sorry . . .

Like, there was this one time when we were

hiking

with

Granddad . . .

I SMELL SMOKE!
I'LL SAVE YOU!

SPLASH
FIZZLE
FIZZLE

H!
OOPS,
SORRY . . .

Then there was that other time when we were at the retirement village

visiting

Great-Aunty Flo . . .

WAIT!
I SMELL SMOKE!
I'LL SAVE YOU!

HAPPY BIRTHDAY TO YOU!
I AM OLD

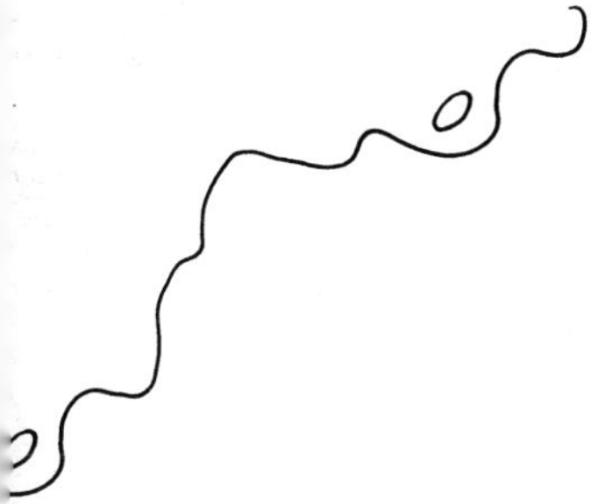

ZZZZHHHHHHHHH

HTHHHHHHHH!
OOPS!
UM, HAPPY BIRTHDAY!

But when there really is an emergency, Dad and his **great nose** will make for one

AWESOME firefighter!

That's right, my dad's training to become **a FIREFIGHTER!**

I've been going to training with him on the weekends. Just to watch. I think it would be a **very cool job**.

Maybe when I grow up and get a bit bigger, I can join him!

We would make the **best** firefighting team!

But to become a firefighter, you have to reach a certain **height**. When they measured Dad, **he just made it!**

Lucky for Dad, he woke up that morning with **really bad bed head**. His **EXTRA-BIG** hair got him just over the line.

Bed head is really just another way of saying

WEIRD HAIR.

My whole family sometimes wakes up with **really funny** bed head.

But the **WORST of all** is Roger!

I often wish I were taller . . . 'cause being short can be **pretty annoying**.

Last year, our family went to the **carnival** and I was **too short** to go on the **big** roller coaster.

They let kids **way younger** than me on the ride, **just** because they were **taller**.

How could they let a **giant baby** on and not me? I think the rule should be:

IF YOU'RE WEARING A DIAPER, STICK TO THE KIDDIE RIDES!

Believe me, **NO ONE** on a roller coaster wants to sit next to someone who's able to

go to the bathroom in their own pants.

And sometimes at the supermarket, I can't reach my **favorite chips!**

They're **always** on the **top shelf!**

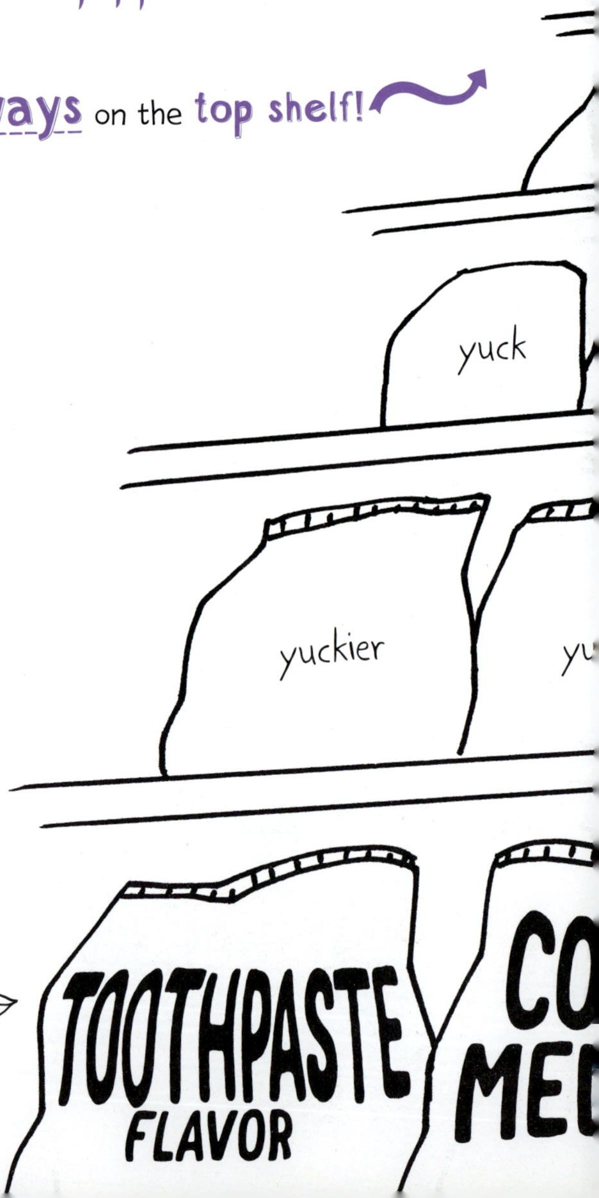

BACON & CHEESE
TOMATO
CHEESY CHEESE
CHICKEN
best chips, way up here
yum
yum
yum
yum
yuck
yuck
yuck
yuckier
yuckier
me! way down here
BRUSSELS SPROUTS
BURP FLAVOR

giant baby!
yuck

BBQ
BACON & CHEESE
TOMATO
CHEESY CHEESE
CHICKEN
best chips, still way up here
yum
yum
yum
yum
yuck
yuck
yuck
yuck
yuckier
yuckier
me, still way down here
BRUSSELS SPROUTS
BURP FLAVOR

Maybe I should **JOIN THE CIRCUS** and learn to walk on stilts.

But I don't know if they'd allow that at the supermarket.

But the **biggest** **problem** with being short is that it makes it hard to play lots of **sports**.

Like

basketball . . .

I wish there were a game called **SHORTBALL**. It'd be **just** like basketball, but the ring would be close to the ground.

All the **BIG GUYS** would **trip** over themselves trying to shoot baskets and the

LITTLE GUYS

would be the CHAMPS!

Who am I kidding?

Life is

pretty tough

for **small guys!**

YEEHAH!

CHAPTER 3

Today, it's **PET DAY** at school! We all get to bring in our pets to show everyone.

It's **funny** how **so many** people **look like their pets**.

Mullet
Ferret
Jenny
Penny

Mary
Scary
Toby Hogan
Hulk Hogan

But then there are others who look

nothing alike.

Like Henry . . .

Then there's
Bella . . .

I thought Bella
would have
something like
a **fluffy** cat . . .

or a **long-eared bunny** . . .

or maybe a little **poodle** . . .

Man,
was I **wrong!**

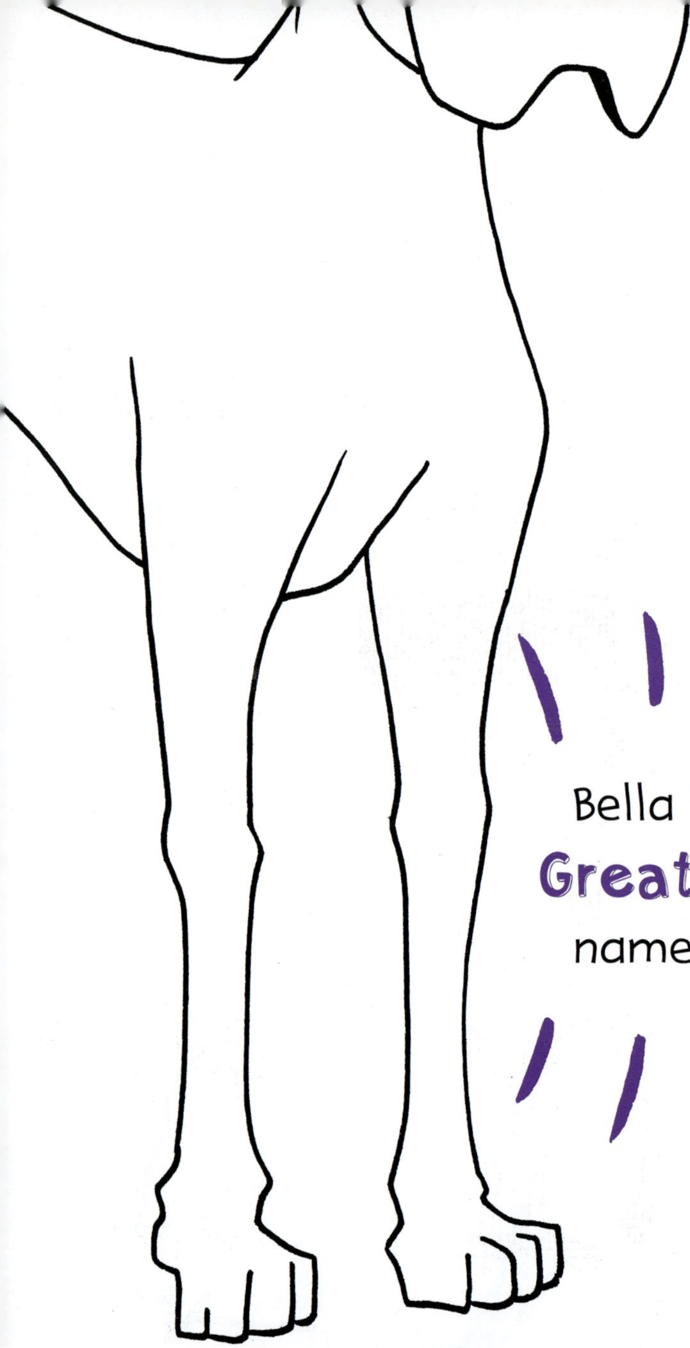

Bella has a **Great Dane** named **Tiny!**

WOW!
GASP!
WOW!

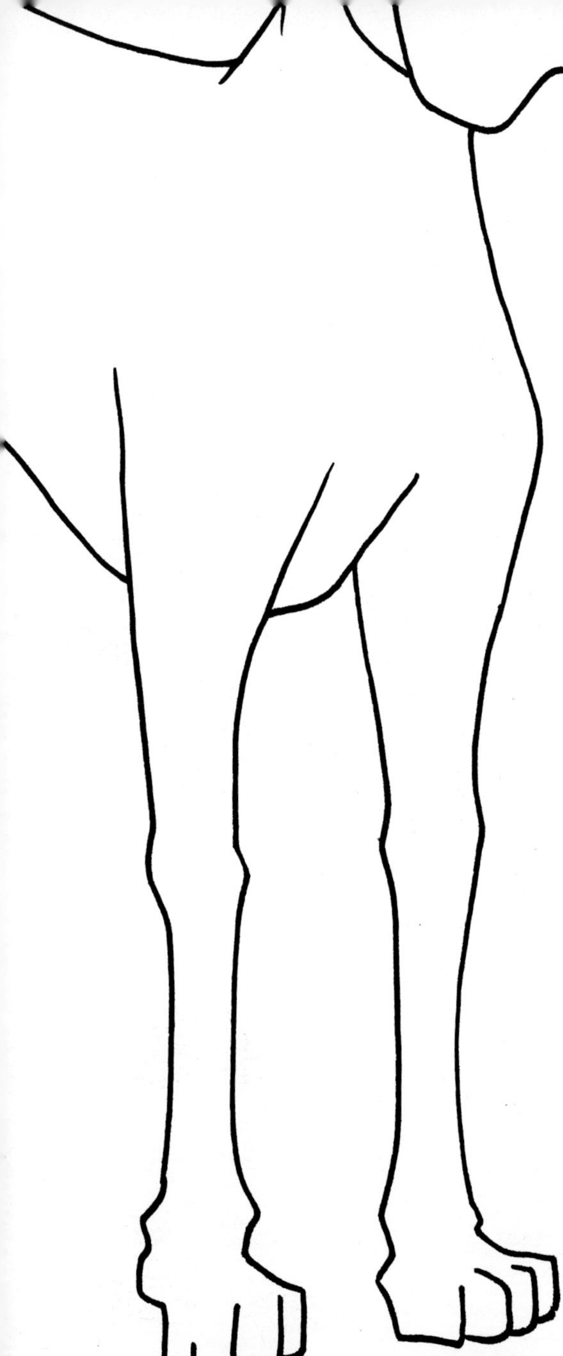

Tiny is **as big as a horse!**

A **really,**

really

BIG horse!

"Um, hi, Tiny," I said, walking up to him.

I'd never felt so small!

"He's friendly," said Bella. "Big, but friendly. Tiny," she said to the dog, "say hello to my friend WeirDo."

WOOO

OOOOOF!

His bark **nearly** blew me **over!**

Bella smiled at me, and I blushed.

"He likes you," said Bella. "I knew he would."

Then Tiny **licked** me!

SLURP!

I was knocked off my feet and landed with a

giant THUD!

Bella helped me up.

SEE! HE REAAAAALLLY LIKES YOU!

That's funny, 'cause I **reaaaaallly** like Bella!

I showed Bella **my** pets.

"You must be FiDo," said Bella, "and you must be Blockhead."

She picked up FiDo and gave him a **cuddle**. Blockhead **jumped** onto her finger and **wriggled**.

Meanwhile, Mr. McDool was rounding up everyone and their pets for the

PET PARADE.

He'd even brought in his own pet!

Everyone lined up with their pets and, **one by one**, we started making our way **around the playground**.

First, Tiny **galloped** along with Bella, and **everyone gasped**.

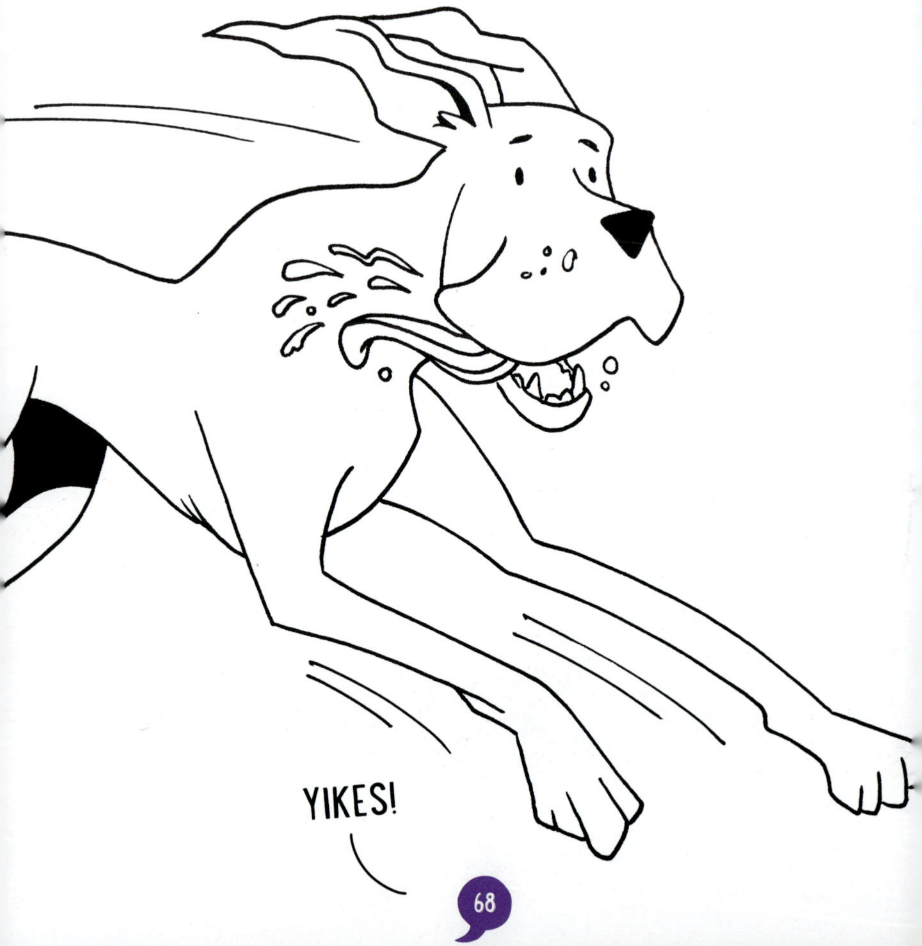

WHOA!
GASP!
YAY!
GO, TINY!

Next, there were Wendy and her **rabbit** hopping backward,

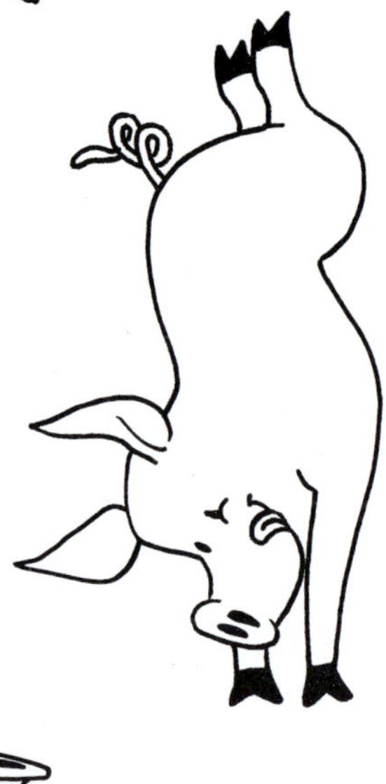

a handstanding **pig**,

and a stunned **goldfish**.

Sally had given me her old **toy pony's saddle** to put on FiDo and a **cowboy hat** to put on Blockhead.

When they ran out with me—

Blockhead riding on the back of FiDo—

everyone laughed like

CRAZY!

And then to top it all off, Blockhead **barked!**

The crowd went **wild!**

After we'd run one lap,

the crowd asked for **MORE!**

So we ran around **again!**

And again!

Henry laughed **so much**
that his juice
shot out
his nose!

FiDo and **Blockhead** were the

STARS

of the

SHOW!

"Quick," said Granddad. "Film them, Weir!"

I turned on the camera

just in time!

STAY TUNED!

CHAPTER 4

Everyone in our family loves hanging out with our pets.

Blockhead and Dad sometimes dance together.

Roger and FiDo love **crawling under things** together.

Blockhead, Mom, and Sally sometimes have **sing-alongs**.

And I **really love** taking Fido for **walks**.

We like walking to the park near our house and playing a game where we **COPY each other**.

When FiDo **rolls over**, I roll over.

When FiDo **pokes his tongue out**, I poke my tongue out.

When FiDo **lies back and sticks his legs in the air**, I lie back and stick my legs in the air.

Just then, I heard a voice . . .

HI, WEIR!
HI, FIDO!

It was **Bella!**

Bella was playing Frisbee with Tiny and asked if we wanted to join in.

Of course we did!

It was **SO MUCH FUN!**

We threw the **Frisbee**

all around

the park!

But then I threw the Frisbee **way too high** and it flew into a tree.

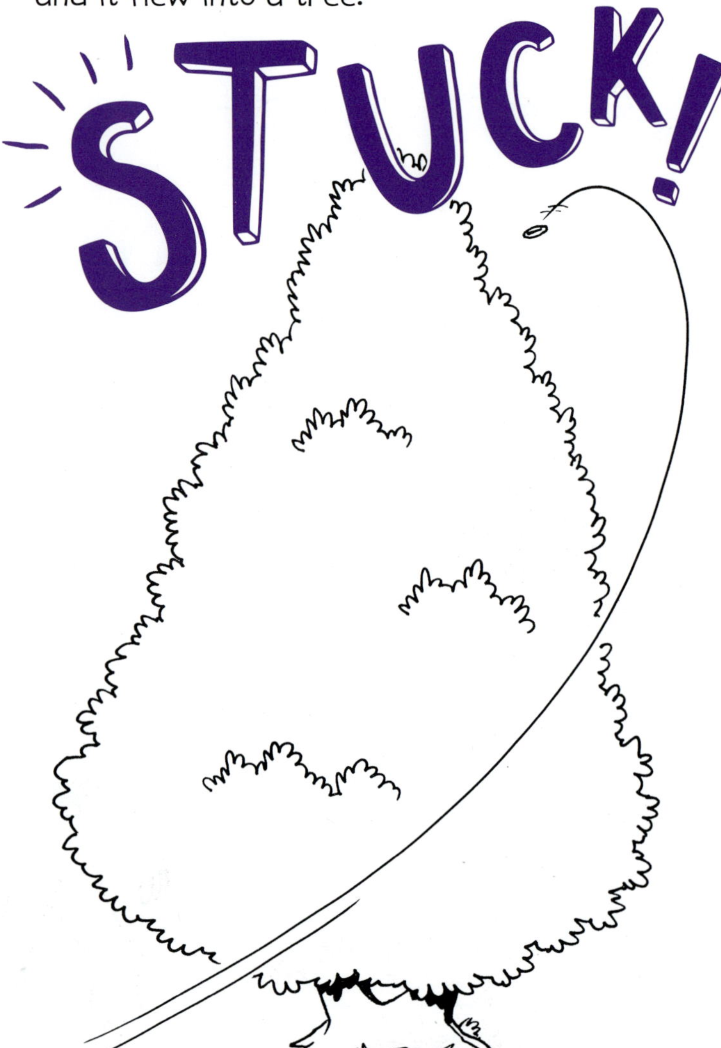

"Oops, sorry, Bella," I said. "You wait here. I'll climb up and get it."

So I **climbed** until I couldn't climb any farther and I reached as **high** as I could!

But I just

couldn't

reach it!

If only I were a **little bit** **taller,** I would have been able to get the Frisbee back for Bella.

"That's okay, Weir," said Bella. "I'll go get my dad, and he'll be able to reach it."

I was **SOOO** embarrassed.

That night at dinner, I was telling Mom and Dad how **I wished I were taller**.

"That's all right," said Dad, "you're still growing."

"Yeah, but I'll never be **really** tall," I said. "If I were taller, I'd be great at basketball."

"You might not be great at basketball, Weir, but you're **really great at other things**," said Mom. "Like . . . **drawing!**"

It was true, I **could** draw.

A

B Fold line B over to meet line A

"Yeah," said Granddad. "And you're really good at **filming things**, too."

"That video you took of Blockhead and FiDo on Pet Day is **really cool**," said Sally. "Who knows, Weir, maybe one day you'll end up being a **famous movie director!**

Imagine that!"

Just then, I came up with a **great idea!**

How cool would it be if they were watching their **favorite TV show** together . . . and then saw themselves on it?!

So Granddad and Sally helped me send in the video.

We could **hardly wait** for the next episode of

Funniest Pets!

FiDo and Blockhead were **SOOO excited** to watch it, and they had **NO IDEA** that we'd sent **their video** to the show!

"Do you think they'll show the video of FiDo and Blockhead?" I asked Dad.

"Let's watch and find out!" said Dad.

As usual, the show was **HILARIOUS!**

There was a **piglet** in mud wearing rubber boots.

There was a **kitten** falling asleep on a piano . . .

and then waking herself up **accidentally!**

And a video of a **hamster** in a tiny hammock, wearing sunglasses.

But **no FIDO** and **no Blockhead** . . .

"Maybe they'll be on next week's show," said Sally.

"Yeah, maybe," I said.

All of a sudden, FiDo and Blockhead both started **barking!**

STAY TUNED,
WE'VE SAVED THE BEST
FOR LAST . . .
STAY TUNED!
HEY,
COOL!

We couldn't believe it! FiDo and Blockhead

WERE ON TV!

NUTS!

CHAPTER 5

In the morning, we woke to **LOUD banging** on the front door.

"Weir, could you please get it?" said Mom. "My hair looks **funny** again."

The banging on the front door kept going.

I climbed out of bed and wandered to the door.

I **couldn't believe** what I found there!

"What's going on?" I asked Henry.

"The video!" he said.

"The video?"

"The video of FiDo and Blockhead on ***Funniest Pets!***" said Henry. "The TV show! **Everyone saw it!** You're famous!"

FAMOUS?

"Uh, I don't know," I said. "I just woke up—"

"There they are!" everyone shouted.

Suddenly, **FiDo** poked his head out of the door and **Blockhead** landed on my shoulder.

The crowd went **nuts**, calling to them and rushing toward us to get a **better look**.

CAMERAS FLASHED.

And flashed.

And flashed.

There was a loud

SQUAWK!

beside me as Blockhead **panicked**.

Oh no.

"Please stop," I called out. "Blockhead doesn't like flashing lights!"

But it was **too late** . . .

BLOCKHEAD, WAIT!

He'd flown away into the sky, far, far away from the flashing cameras . . . and

far,

far

away

from home!

WUFF
WUFF!

CHAPTER 6

We **searched all day** for Blockhead, but couldn't find him **anywhere!**

Henry and **Mo** joined in.

Bella and **Tiny**, too.

We looked in **all of his favorite places**.

We checked the **creek** where we sometimes take him for a bird bath.

We checked the **bird shop** where we buy his birdseed.

We even checked the **TV shop** where Blockhead and FiDo sometimes like to watch TV.

Sally and Henry helped me put up some **Missing posters**.

LOST BIRD

Answers to Blockhead, Blockie, and Hey, Bird!

LIKES: Wriggling, mooing, barking. Most of all, likes playing with his best friend, FiDo.

DOESN'T LIKE: Flashing lights.

REWARD: Anything you like from Henry's pet rock collection.

I was **really worried** about Blockhead. I could tell FiDo was, too. He kept **wuff-wuffing**, calling out to his friend.

"It'll be okay," said Bella. "You'll find him."

"I hope so," I replied.

"Woof!" said Tiny.

Then he gave me and Fido

a **HUGE** lick.

WRIGGLE!

CHAPTER 7

Dad unbolted the shed, and we took a look inside.

We found a few **daddy longlegs** . . .

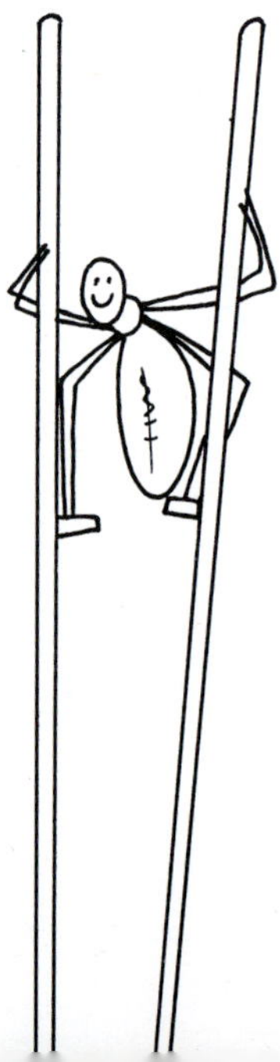

and even one **daddy short legs**!

But there was **no sign of a dog**!

We were thinking he must have found a way out, when we heard **barking**!

We looked inside again . . . but there was **definitely no dog in there!**

Just the spiders!

We'd just about **run out of ideas**, when we realized FIDO had wandered off.

We found him **wriggling** behind the back of the shed.

"FiDo, come back, boy," called Dad.

But FiDo **wriggled in farther**.

"FiDo," I called.

But he'd **already disappeared** behind the shed.

“What is it, FiDo?” I called out. “What have you found back there?”

Dad tried to follow him . . .

He **tried** . . .

and **tried** . . .

. . . and tried!

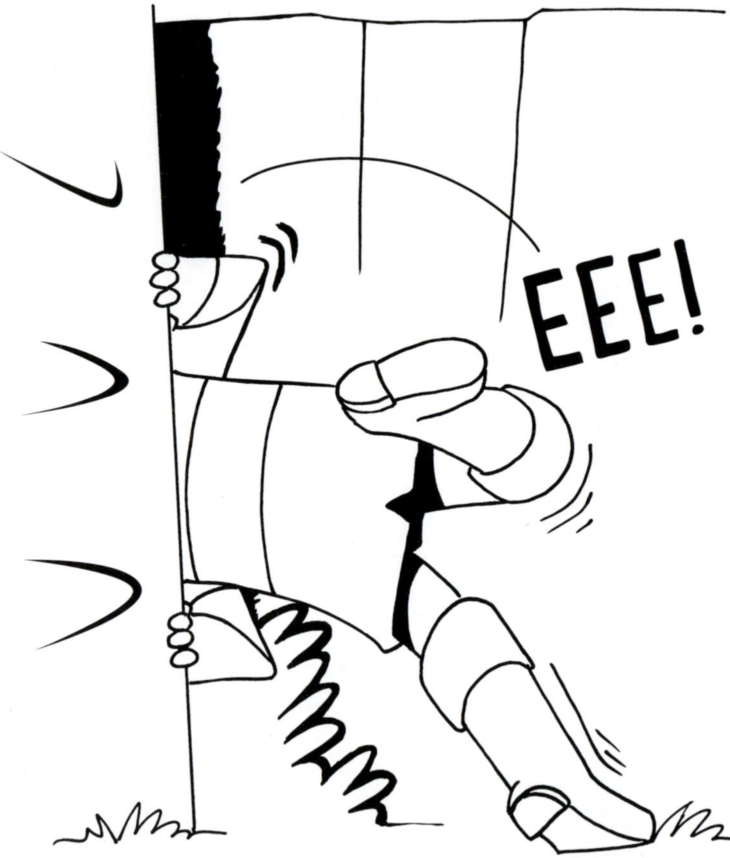

But no amount of **wriggling** was going to **squeeze** him through!

I suddenly realized that **I could fit** through!

"Dad, can I try?" I asked.

"Sure thing, Weir!"

Dad stepped out of the way, and I began **wriggling** behind the shed.

Wriggling behind the shed was **easy for me** . . . I guess **being small helps sometimes!**

You **wouldn't believe** who I found back there!
TA-DA!
WOOF! WOOF!
WUFF! WUFF!

There was no dog!

It was **Blockhead** who was **barking** all along!

TO THE RESCUE!

CHAPTER 8

Blockhead had hurt his wing flying behind the school shed, but he's **much better** already.

Everyone's been helping him rest up.

Especially FiDo and me.

Dad thinks I'll make an **awesome** firefighter one day. And maybe even FiDo could join me as a **rescue dog**.

TO THE RESCUE!

For Summer Do

FROM ANH

the 4th

little Weirdo!

DEDICATIONS

FROM JULES

For my mum and dad,
who encouraged me to be
anything I wanted,
as long as I gave it my best.

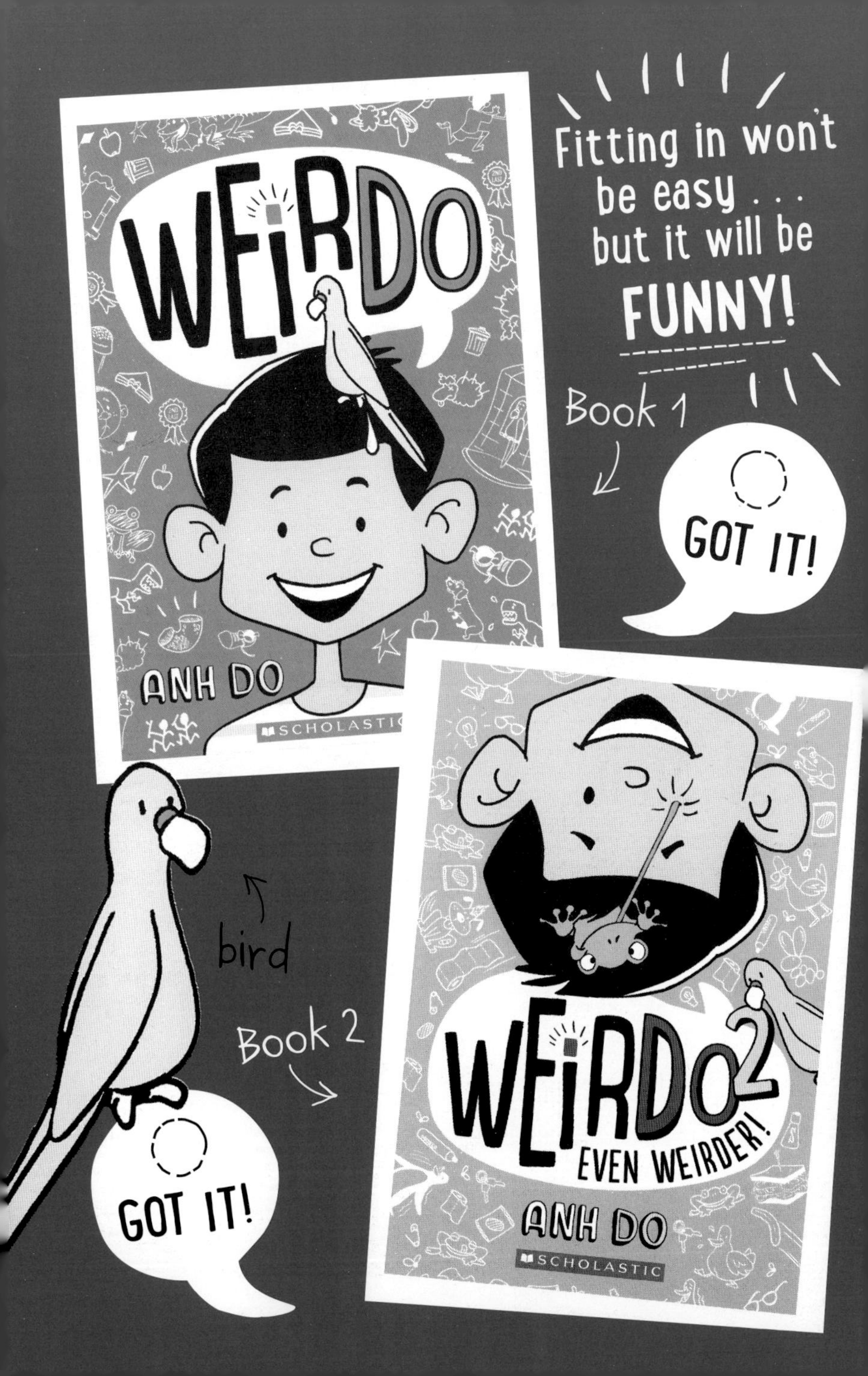
WEiRDO
ANH DO
SCHOLASTIC
Fitting in won't be easy . . . but it will be FUNNY!
Book 1
GOT IT!
bird
Book 2
GOT IT!
WEiRDO 2
EVEN WEIRDER!
ANH DO
SCHOLASTIC

COLLECT THEM ALL!

YOU CAN NEVER HAVE TOO MANY WEIRDOS

Book 3

GOT IT!

Book 4

GOT IT!

STAY TUNED!